101 Super Cool Ice Cream Treats

by Lisa deMauro
illustrations by Jerry Zimmerman

PARACHUTE
PRESS, INC.

Parachute Press, Inc.
156 Fifth Avenue
New York, NY 10010

Copyright © 1989 Parachute Press, Inc.
ISBN: 0-938753-23-1

First printing: April 1989
Printed in the USA

Design by R. D'Anna

INTRODUCTION

No doubt, you are an ice cream lover. (If you're not, you've got the wrong book!) In fact, we are a nation of ice cream lovers. On the average, we *each* eat about eighteen pounds of ice cream a year. And while some people eat less, some people—you know who you are—eat more!

Even though we've got hundreds of flavors to choose from, we still love good old vanilla best. (Chocolate is our second favorite, and strawberry is our favorite fruit flavor.)

So, ice cream lover, what do you need a recipe book for? After all, anyone with a spoon knows what to do with ice cream. (If you've got a cone, you don't even *need* the spoon!)

You need this book to show you a few ice cream tricks that you probably don't know — like, how to make a Classic Chocolate Milk Shake. Or a Peanut Cream Dream. Or a Polar Bear in a Snowstorm.

So pull up a bowl, a spoon, and some of the cold stuff, and dig in. If you love ice cream, you've got a treat in store . . . 101 treats!

Table of Contents

ABOUT USING THIS BOOK

Most of the recipes in this book call for chocolate or vanilla ice cream. Try the recipes as they're written, or make your own versions using macadamia nut fudge or raspberry ripple or whatever sounds good. After all, if it's made with ice cream, how bad can it be?

Before you begin, remember: *Always* get permission to make any treat, and ask an adult to stay nearby when you are creating — just in case you need help.

A is for
AFTER SCHOOL SNACKS

These snacks fit perfectly into that after-school and before-dinner time. They're something to look forward to as you head home after a day of serious brain work.

#1 ICY BITES

These mini-sandwiches are fun to make *and* to eat with friends.

You need:

> 1 scoop of ice cream (any
>   flavor) soft enough to spread
> a few handfuls of animal
>   crackers or little bear cookies

Put one large scoop of ice cream into a bowl. Spread a little ice cream on the back of a cookie. Top with another cookie. Eat. Makes a bunch.

#2 MUFFIN MAGIC

Instead of butter, try a dab of ice cream magic on your muffin. If the muffin's hot, it's twice as magical.

You need:

> 1 muffin, any kind
> 1 or 2 tablespoons vanilla ice
> cream

Slice off the top of the muffin. Ask an adult to warm the muffin in a microwave for 15-30 seconds, or toast it in a toaster oven.

Spread each side of the muffin with ice cream. Let it sit about 1 minute. Dig in. MMMMmmm! Makes 1.

#3 PEANUT BUTTER SECRET

Great Moment in Ice Cream History: As ice cream legend has it, the ice cream cone was invented at the St. Louis Exposition of 1904 when an ice cream vendor ran out of dishes. How can you sell ice cream with nothing to put it in? Next door to the ice cream vendor was a waffle salesman. The vendor bought waffles from the salesman, rolled them into a cone shape, and filled them up with ice cream! People ate up the new creation!

You'll eat up this creation, too. The cone has a secret inside.

You need:

> 1 sugar cone
> 1 tablespoon peanut butter
> (smooth or chunky)
> 1-2 teaspoons chocolate chips
> (milk chocolate or
> semisweet)
> 1 scoop chocolate ice cream

Use a butter knife to coat the inside of a sugar cone with peanut butter. Sprinkle a few chocolate chips into the cone. Put about a teaspoon of chocolate ice cream into the cone. Push it down. Sprinkle on a few more chocolate chips. Add another teaspoon of ice cream, followed by the rest of the chocolate chips. Top it off with the rest of the ice cream. Eat. Makes 1.

#4 MONDAY SUNDAE

When you get up on Monday morning, think about coming home to this.

You need:
- 1 tablespoon peanut butter
- 1 teaspoon jam, jelly, or preserves (any flavor)
- 1-2 teaspoons milk
- 1 scoop vanilla ice cream
- 1 teaspoon chopped peanuts, (optional)

Put the peanut butter, jam, and 1 teaspoon milk into a small bowl. (A 1-cup measure with a handle makes a good bowl.) Mash and stir until the mixture is a well-blended sauce. (The jam will probably leave little lumps, but that's okay. If your sauce is too thick, add a little more milk and stir some more.)

Put vanilla ice cream in a dish. Spoon the peanut butter and jelly sauce over the ice cream. Top with a few chopped peanuts. Eat. Makes 1.

B is for
BANANA SPLITS

#5 BANANA BARGE

Try to use a long, narrow dish for this treat.

You need:

- 1 large banana
- 1 scoop each of vanilla and chocolate ice cream
- chocolate syrup
- marshmallow topping
- whipped cream
- 2 maraschino cherries

Ask an adult to help you cut the banana lengthwise in quarters, so that you have four long pieces. Place them in a long, narrow dish. (If you don't have a long dish, cut the pieces in half crosswise and stand them around the edge of a dessert bowl.)

Put 1 scoop each of vanilla and chocolate ice cream, side-by-side, on top of the bananas. Pour some chocolate syrup over the vanilla ice cream. Spoon marshmallow topping over the chocolate ice cream. (Thin the topping with a few drops of water or milk if it's too thick.) Cover with whipped cream and put 2 cherries on top. Enjoy! Makes 1.

#6 BANANA ROYALE

Just one of these is enough for you — and maybe a friend or two!

You need:

> 2 medium bananas
> 1 scoop each vanilla, chocolate,
>   and strawberry ice cream
> chocolate syrup
> butterscotch topping
> marshmallow topping
> pineapple chunks or sliced
>   strawberries
> whipped cream
> chopped nuts

Ask an adult to help you slice 2 medium bananas in half crosswise, then cut the halves into quarters lengthwise. (You'll have 16 pieces of banana.) Lay the banana pieces across the bottom and around the sides of a large dessert bowl. Cover with 1 scoop each of vanilla, chocolate, and strawberry ice cream. Spoon or pour the chocolate syrup, marshmallow topping, and butterscotch topping over each scoop of ice cream. (Thin the toppings with a few drops of water or milk, if they're too thick.) Spoon on sliced strawberries or pineapple chunks. Cover with whipped cream. Sprinkle chopped nuts on top. Attack! Makes 1.

C is for CHOCOLATE

#7 CHOCOLATE TRIPLE THREAT

Proceed with caution: this is *serious* chocolate!

You need:

> 1 chocolate brownie without
> icing
> 1 scoop chocolate ice cream
> 1 tablespoon chocolate syrup
> whipped cream
> chocolate sprinkles (jimmies)

Put a chocolate brownie on a plate. Top with a scoop of chocolate ice cream. Cover with chocolate syrup. Then top it all with whipped cream and a few chocolate sprinkles. Eat if you dare! Makes 1.

#8 BLACK HOLE CONE

You could get lost in this one!

You need:

1 cone (sugar or waffle)
2-4 teaspoons hot fudge
    topping from a jar (or any
    thick chocolate sauce)
2-3 teaspoons chopped nuts
1 scoop chocolate ice cream
chocolate sprinkles (jimmies)

Put about ½ teaspoon hot fudge topping into an empty cone. (Don't heat it up first.) Sprinkle in some nuts. Spoon in about 1 teaspoon chocolate ice cream. Push the ice cream down into the cone. Put in layers of fudge topping, nuts, and ice cream, until you reach the top of the cone. Then finish off with a mound of ice cream. Top with chocolate sprinkles. Dig in. Makes 1.

#9 HOT FUDGE CHOCOLATE DREAM

When you can't get enough chocolate, try this.

You need:

> 1 large scoop chocolate ice cream
> 2 chocolate sandwich cookies with white filling
> about 1/2 recipe hot fudge sauce (see #58, HOT FUDGE SUNDAE)

Put 1 large scoop chocolate ice cream into a dessert bowl. Crumble 1 chocolate sandwich cookie over the ice cream. Top with hot fudge sauce. Crumble another chocolate sandwich cookie on top. Dive in. Makes 1.

#10 CHOCO-CREAM FIZZ

A chocolate-y drink for your sweet tooth!

You need:

> 2-3 tablespoons chocolate syrup
> 6-8 ounces cream soda
> 2-3 scoops chocolate ice cream

Pour 2 tablespoons chocolate syrup into a glass. Add a few tablespoons cream soda and stir until the syrup is mixed in. Drop in 2 or 3 scoops chocolate ice cream. Top off the glass with cream soda — watch out for the fizz! Stir it up and drink. Makes 1.

#11 LIQUID PEANUT BUTTER CUP

You'll love it — peanut butter and chocolate all shook up!

You need:

        1-2 tablespoons peanut butter
        3-4 tablespoons chocolate
          syrup
        ½ cup milk
        3 scoops chocolate ice cream

Put 1-2 tablespoons peanut butter in a big glass (or a milk shake machine container or blender). Add 3-4 tablespoons chocolate syrup. Stir until the mixture is smooth. Add ½ cup milk and stir well. Then add 3 scoops chocolate ice cream. Stir (or whirl in the machine) until the ice cream is mixed in, but not completely melted. The consistency should be thick and frothy. Drink. Makes 1 tall shake.

D is for
DO-IT-YOURSELF
ICE CREAM

Great Moment in Ice Cream History: An American, Nancy Johnson, invented the hand-cranked ice cream freezer that is still used by people today. A turning paddle (called a "dasher") keeps the ice cream mixture in motion while it sits surrounded by icy salted water. (Ice cream needs temperatures lower than 32 degrees Fahrenheit to freeze. But pure ice cannot get colder than 32 degrees. Salt lowers the temperature of ice. That's why salted icy water, or brine, is used to make ice cream. But some modern machines don't use ice at all.)

Before Ms. Johnson's invention, ice cream making was hard work. Based on Ms. Johnson's invention, almost *anyone* can make ice cream almost *anywhere!*

Of course you can always *buy* ice cream, but making it, with these recipes, is half the fun.

#12 VANILLA ICE CREAM

You have to use an ice cream maker for this recipe.
You need:

> **1 cup heavy (whipping) cream**
> **⅓ cup sugar**
> **1 cup milk**
> **2 teaspoons vanilla extract**

Pour 1 cup heavy cream into a small sauce pan. Ask an adult to warm the cream over low heat until little bubbles begin to appear around the edge. With a pot holder, remove the pan from heat. Stir in ⅓ cup sugar, until sugar is dissolved. Carefully pour the mixture into a small mixing bowl. Refrigerate until the mixture is chilled. (If your refrigerator has glass shelves, put a pot holder under the bowl.)

After chilling, stir in 1 cup milk and 2 teaspoons vanilla extract. Freeze in an ice cream maker according to the manufacturer's instructions. Serve. Makes 1 pint.

#13 MIXING BOWL VANILLA

Make this ice cream *without* a machine! It's rich and yummy.

You need:

> 1 cup heavy (whipping) cream
> ²/₃ cup (half of a 14-ounce can)
> sweetened condensed milk
> (don't use evaporated milk)
> 2 teaspoons vanilla extract
> ½ cup milk

In a small mixing bowl, use a hand mixer to whip the heavy cream until it is thick — but *not* so thick that when you lift the beaters it stands in tall peaks. Put the bowl in the freezer for about ½ hour or until the cream begins to freeze on top and around the edges.

Use the mixer to beat in the sweetened condensed milk and vanilla extract. Beat until the mixture is thick enough to make little ridges in the surface. Freeze 1 hour.

Beat in ½ cup milk. Return to the freezer for about 2 hours, until firm. Serve. Makes 1 pint.

#14 CHOCOLATE SYRUP ICE CREAM I

Make this treat *with* an ice cream maker.

You need:

> 1 cup heavy (whipping) cream
> 1 cup milk
> 1 cup chocolate syrup
> 1 teaspoon vanilla extract

Mix all the ingredients together in a bowl until smooth. Chill about one hour. Pour mixture into ice cream maker and follow manufacturer's directions. Makes about 1½ pints.

#15 CHOCOLATE SYRUP ICE CREAM II

Make this treat *without* an ice cream maker.

Follow the directions for making CHOCOLATE SYRUP ICE CREAM I. After mixing the ingredients in a bowl, pour the mixture into a plastic container, cover tightly, and freeze about 1 hour. Stir the mixture to break up the ice crystals. Cover and freeze for another hour. Stir well again. Then freeze until firm, about 2 hours. Makes about 1 pint.

E is for
EASY AS PIE

You can buy crumb crusts in the baking section of your supermarket, or make your own. Most graham cracker boxes and some chocolate cookie packages have recipes for crusts — or check a cookbook.

#16 MISSISSIPPI MUD PIE

The "mud" in this pie is fudge sauce.

You need:

> 2 pints strawberry ice cream
> 1 chocolate cookie or graham
>   cracker crumb pie shell
> 1 jar hot fudge sauce

Put the ice cream in the refrigerator for about 10 minutes or until you can spread it easily. Don't let it get soupy. Spoon the ice cream into the pie shell. Spread it evenly. Smooth the top. Freeze the pie 30-60 minutes or until the ice cream is very hard. Spoon the fudge sauce over the ice cream. (Don't heat the sauce first.) Serve, or return the pie to the freezer until you are ready.
Serves 8-10.

#17 MISSISSIPPI MINT PIE

A minty-cool version of the MISSISSIPPI MUD PIE.

You need:

> 2 pints mint chocolate chip ice cream
>
> 1 chocolate cookie or graham cracker crumb pie shell
> chocolate mint sauce (see #59, WORTH-A-MINT SUNDAE, for recipe)
> handful of crushed peppermint candies

Follow directions for MISSISSIPPI MUD PIE. While the ice cream is freezing in the pie shell, make the chocolate mint sauce, following the directions in treat #59. As you let the sauce cool to room temperature, stir from time to time so it will be smooth. Spread the cooled sauce on the frozen pie. Sprinkle crushed peppermint candies over the top. Serve or store in freezer until you are ready to eat. Serves 8-10.

#18 ORANGE SILK PIE

This pie is smooth as silk!

You need:

>
> 1 14-ounce can sweetened
>   condensed milk
> 1 cup evaporated milk
> 1/4 cup lemon juice
> 1 6-ounce can frozen orange
>   juice concentrate
> 1 graham cracker or chocolate
>   cookie crumb pie shell
> unpeeled slices from one
>   seedless orange
> whipped cream

Pour the condensed milk, evaporated milk, lemon juice, and frozen orange juice concentrate into a mixing bowl. Ask an adult to beat the mixture with an electric mixer until smooth. Pour mixture into pie shell. Make room in the freezer for the pie to sit flat with nothing on top of it. Freeze 2-3 hours or until smooth.

Cut the orange slices in half. When you're ready to serve, place orange pieces around the edge of the pie for decoration. Serve with whipped cream. Makes 6-10 servings.

F is for FLOATS

Great Moment in Ice Cream History: The ice cream float was born in 1874, when a Philadelphia soda fountain attendant dropped some ice cream into a glass of soda by mistake. How's that for a yummy mishap?

#19 BLACK AND WHITE: Pour 2-4 tablespoons chocolate syrup into a tall glass. Add 2 scoops vanilla ice cream. Fill with club soda or seltzer. Stir.

#20 WHITE AND BLACK: Put 2 scoops chocolate ice cream into a tall glass. Add cream soda.

#21 MIDNIGHT: Pour 2-4 tablespoons chocolate syrup into a tall glass. Add 2 scoops chocolate ice cream. Fill with club soda or seltzer. Stir.

#22 CHERRY PICKER: Put 2 scoops vanilla ice cream into a tall glass. Add cherry cola.

#23 BLACK COW: Put 2 scoops vanilla ice cream into a tall glass. Add root beer.

#24 CHOCOLATE COW: Put 2 tablespoons chocolate syrup into a tall glass. Add 2 scoops chocolate ice cream. Fill with root beer. Stir.

#25 BROWN BULL: Put 2 scoops chocolate ice cream into a tall glass. Add cola.

#26 PURPLE COW: Put 2-4 tablespoons frozen grape juice concentrate into a tall glass. Add 2 scoops vanilla ice cream. Fill with ginger ale. Stir.

To get the most out of your float (also called an ice cream soda), use a straw *and* a spoon!

G is for
GOURMET TREATS

Great Moment in Ice Cream History: Dolly Madison elevated the status of ice cream when she served it at a state dinner at the White House during the early 1800s.

If it worked for Dolly, it will work for you. Serve these recipes when you're entertaining grown-ups, or when you want a real gourmet treat.

#27 PEACH MELBA

It's the raspberry sauce that makes this treat so special!
You need:

> 1 10-ounce can frozen
>   raspberries in syrup, thawed
> 2 scoops vanilla ice cream
> 2 canned peach halves

Pour the thawed raspberries in syrup into a blender or food processor. An adult should blend the berries until they are completely crushed. Place a strainer over a bowl so that it sits securely on the rim. (Make sure the bowl is large enough to hold the strained raspberries.) Pour the raspberry mixture into the strainer. Stir and mash the mixture to push it through the strainer. (Most of the seeds should stay in the strainer.) Set aside.

Put 2 scoops vanilla ice cream into a dessert bowl. Cover each scoop with a canned peach half, pitted side down. Pour raspberry sauce over the peaches and serve. Makes 1 plus lots of sauce.

#28 PEARS HELENE

This treat is like a banana split, but with pears instead of bananas!

You need:

> 2 canned pear halves
> 2 scoops vanilla ice cream
> 2-4 tablespoons chocolate
> syrup

Put 2 pear halves into a dessert bowl, pitted side up. Cover each half with a scoop of vanilla ice cream. Pour chocolate syrup over all. Serve. Makes 1.

#29 STRAWBERRY SHORTCAKE

This is a cool version of an old favorite.

You need:

> 1/2 cup sliced strawberries
> 1 teaspoon sugar
> 1 large or 2 small slices of
> poundcake
> 1 scoop vanilla ice cream
> a large dollop of whipped cream

Put strawberries into a small bowl. Pick the biggest and juiciest berry and set it aside. Sprinkle remaining berries with sugar. Mash them lightly with a fork to make them a bit juicy. Set aside for 30 minutes.

After 30 minutes, put the poundcake in a dessert bowl. Cover with half the sliced strawberries plus any juice in the bowl. Scoop vanilla ice cream over the berries. Spoon on the rest of the berries. Top with whipped cream. Place your choice berry on top. Serve. Makes 1.

H is for
HOT AND COOL

Ice cream is oh so cool and creamy, especially when it just starts to melt under a pool of hot topping.

#30 MAPLE STICKIES

You need *real* maple syrup for this (not maple-flavored syrup). Kids in Vermont used to make candy with hot syrup and clean snow. This is an ice cream version of that sweet treat. CAUTION: This is not for people who wear braces!

You need:
> 2 tablespoons real maple syrup
> ½ cup vanilla ice cream

Spoon ice cream into individual teaspoon-sized lumps on a small sturdy plate. (Don't use the good china.) Place in freezer.

Pour the maple syrup into a very small saucepan. Ask an adult to warm it over low heat. Be careful: it will boil quickly and get *very* hot. You'll see bubbles around the edge of the syrup right away. When the whole surface is covered with big bubbles, time it for 2 minutes. With a pot holder, remove from heat.

Take the ice cream lumps out of the freezer.

Drizzle the hot maple syrup over each lump. The syrup will harden and be sticky. Eat right away, but don't burn your mouth! Makes 1 serving.

#31 BROWNIE FAKED ALASKA

Great Moment in Ice Cream History: Thomas Jefferson was a *big* ice cream fan. When he was ambassador to France, he heard about a new ice cream sensation. It was Jefferson who introduced this sensation—ice cream topped with meringue, now known as Baked Alaska—to the United States.

This recipe is a "Faked" Alaska because instead of using egg whites for the traditional meringue topping, we use marshmallow cream.

You need:

- 2 heaping tablespoons fluffy marshmallow cream
- vegetable shortening spray
- 1 scoop chocolate ice cream, soft enough to spread
- 1 brownie, about 3" square

Cut a sheet of aluminum foil about 10-12 inches long. Spray the sheet with a coating of vegetable shortening and fold it in half. Unfold the foil. Put the marshmallow cream in a mound to the left of the center line on the foil. Fold the foil over the cream and press gently until the cream spreads out into a circle or oval about ¼" thick. (This doesn't have to be at all exact.) Put the cream in the freezer for 30 minutes or more.

Put a brownie on a piece of foil and place the foil on a cookie sheet (or use the tray of a toaster oven, lined with foil). Spread 1 scoop of chocolate ice cream evenly over the brownie. Freeze.

When 30 minutes have passed, take the marshmallow cream from the freezer. Unfold the foil and carefully peel off the marshmallow. (If it tears, you can pinch it together.) Drape it over the ice cream on top of the brownie. Be sure it completely covers the ice cream and some or all of the brownie.

Ask an adult to put the "Alaska" under the broiler or in a toaster oven set to "Top Brown." Broil until the marshmallow just begins to turn color — between 45 seconds and 2 minutes. Watch carefully. Remove and eat. Makes 1.

#32 S'MORE S'MERRIER

Great Moment in Ice Cream History: President George Washington liked ice cream so much that during the summer of 1790, he bought $200 worth!

If you're making this recipe during the summer, you can use a barbecue. Otherwise, the kitchen stove will do.

You need:

> **1 marshmallow**
> **1 heaping tablespoon chocolate ice cream**
> **2 small graham cracker squares (1 whole rectangular cracker, broken in half)**

Spread the chocolate ice cream on 1 graham cracker square. Place in freezer. Ask an adult to help you toast 1 marshmallow over a barbecue or kitchen stove. Use a skewer or a fork with a wooden handle. The skewer or fork may get hot so carefully remove the toasted marshmallow, and put it on top of the chocolate ice cream. Cover with the other graham cracker square and squish. Eat. Makes 1.

#33 FROZEN HOT CHOCOLATE

This cup of cocoa is perfect for a hot summer's day!

You need:

> 4 heaping teaspoons
>   unsweetened cocoa powder
> 1 cup plus 2 tablespoons water
> 1 14-ounce can sweetened
>   condensed milk (not
>   evaporated milk)

Put the cocoa powder into a small mixing bowl. Add 2 tablespoons water and mix well until there are no more lumps of cocoa powder. Add condensed milk and stir. Add the rest of the water and mix well. Pour mixture into 4 paper cups and freeze 2-3 hours or until firm. "Drink" these with a spoon! Makes 4.

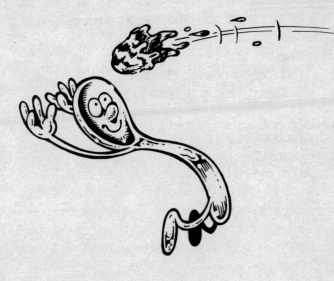

I is for
ICE AND EASY

Great Moments in Ice Cream History: Before ice cream, there were ices. Three thousand years ago the Chinese mixed snow and fruit juices to make ice desserts. Later, Marco Polo brought recipes for water and milk ices to Italy, from China. And fruit ices were popular in the French court during the sixteenth century.

Ices, sherbets, and sorbets are made with flavoring, water, and sugar. Because they're not full of cream, they're lighter and more refreshing than ice cream. You can use ice, sherbet, or sorbet for the recipes below.

#34 ORANGE SUNRISE

This is a fancy way to start the day. It's perfect for a birthday breakfast.

You need:

> 1 scoop orange sherbet
> about ½ cup orange juice

Put a scoop of orange sherbet into a juice glass. (Use a fancy stemmed glass if you can!) Fill the glass with orange juice. Serve with a small spoon. Makes 1.

#35 SNOWBERRY CUP

This treat is easy to make, but it looks very elegant.

You need:

> 2 scoops raspberry sherbet
> a big dollop of whipped cream
> 2 heaping tablespoons fresh or
>   thawed frozen raspberries or
>   sliced strawberries
> butter cookie for decoration

Put raspberry sherbet into a dessert bowl. Top with a big dollop of whipped cream. Spoon the raspberries over the cream. Stick a butter cookie into the sherbet. Eat. Makes 1.

#36 PUCKER UPPER

This is the right stuff for a hot summer day!

You need:

> 1 scoop *each* orange, lemon,
> and lime sherbet
> 6-8 ounces lemonade

Stack orange, lemon, and lime sherbet in a tall glass.
Add lemonade to cover. Drink. Makes 1.

J is for
JELLY, JAM, AND JELL-O

#37 DONUT JAMMIE

Turn a plain donut into a jelly donut with a c-o-o-o-l
difference.

You need:

> 1 plain donut
> 1-2 tablespoons jam or jelly
> 2-4 tablespoons vanilla ice
> cream

Ask an adult to slice a plain donut in half so that you
have two circles. Spread your favorite jam or jelly over
the cut side of each half. Spoon the vanilla ice cream
over one of the jam-covered halves. Top with the other
jam-covered half. Eat. Makes 1.

#38 CHERRY BOMBS

It's the Jell-O that keeps these bombs from freezing
too hard.

You need:

> 1 box cherry-flavored Jell-O
> 1 cup boiling water
> ¾ cup vanilla or cherry vanilla
> ice cream
> 4 7-ounce paper or plastic cups
> 2 cups whipped cream or
> whipped topping
> 4 maraschino cherries

33

Empty 1 box cherry Jell-O into a small bowl. (A metal bowl is best, since it shortens the chilling time.) Ask an adult to add 1 cup boiling water to the mix. Stir until the powder is dissolved. Refrigerate until the mixture is cool (about 25-30 minutes) but not until it is solid. (If it sets before you're ready for it, set the bowl in a large bowl of warm water and stir until the Jell-O is liquid again. Then cool in the refrigerator and proceed.)

Spoon the ice cream into the Jell-O, breaking the ice cream into small pieces. Stir. The ice cream will melt into the mixture, making marble swirls. As the ice cream melts, the mixture will thicken. When the ice cream is thoroughly blended, spoon the mixture into 4 7-ounce paper or plastic cups. Make the tops level. Freeze until very firm — at least 1 hour.

When you're ready to serve, dip each cup into hot water for 10 seconds. Pop the frozen mounds onto plates. Let them sit at room temperature up to 15 minutes. Cover each mound with whipped cream. Top with a cherry. Serve. Makes 4.

#39 RAINBOW SUNDAE

Treat your eyes *and* your mouth to this recipe!
> *You need:*
>> 2 scoops ice cream
>> 2-4 tablespoons each of any *2*
>> flavors of Jell-O, jam, or jelly

If you're using Jell-O, chop it into small chunks. Put 2 scoops of ice cream side-by-side in a dessert bowl. Spoon some Jell-O, jam, or jelly over one scoop of ice cream. Spoon another flavor of Jell-O, jam, or jelly over the other scoop of ice cream. Eat. Makes 1.

K is for KIDS ONLY

Try out these mixtures. You can always pour the syrups and toppings on one at a time, but mixing them all together is half the fun.

For these treats you need a serious sweet tooth!

#40 CHOCOLATE GOO

Put a heaping tablespoon of marshmallow topping into a cup or small bowl. Add 1-2 teaspoons of chocolate syrup. Mix. If it's too thick, add a few drops of milk and mix some more. (Don't add too much milk at once.) Spoon over your favorite ice cream.

#41 PEANUT BUTTER GLOP

Follow directions for CHOCOLATE GOO using 1 heaping tablespoon *each* of peanut butter and marshmallow topping for your ingredients.

#42 BUTTERSCOTCH GLUE

Follow directions for CHOCOLATE GOO using 1 heaping tablespoon of marshmallow topping and 1 heaping teaspoon of butterscotch topping for your ingredients.

#43 SUPERGOO PIE

Gooey, gloppy, and gluey.

You need:

> 1 cup marshmallow cream
> 1/2 cup peanut butter
> 1/4 cup chocolate syrup
> 1/4 cup butterscotch topping
> 1 cup milk
> 1 graham cracker crumb
>   pie shell
> vanilla ice cream

Make room in the freezer for a pie to sit flat with nothing on top of it. Put the marshmallow cream, peanut butter, chocolate syrup, and butterscotch topping in a mixing bowl. Ask an adult to mix them together with an electric beater. If the mixture is too stiff to mix, add some of the milk, 1 tablespoon at a time, until the mixture is smooth. Then slowly add the rest of the milk, beating continuously, until it is all mixed in.

Pour into pie shell and freeze until firm, about 2 hours. Top with vanilla ice cream and serve. Makes 6-10 servings.

L is for LIGHT DELIGHTS

These recipes are perfect for those times when you've got to have *something*, but you don't want *too much*. Mix and match, or make up your own de*lights*!

To drink:

#44 COLA FLOAT: Sugar-free cola with a scoop of chocolate ice milk.

#45 GINGERBERRY: Sugar-free ginger ale with a scoop of strawberry ice milk.

#46 VANILLA SLIM: Skim or lowfat milk whirled with a scoop of vanilla ice milk and a teaspoon of vanilla extract.

#47 SUN SODA: Sugar-free orange soda with a scoop of orange sherbet.

To eat out of hand:

#48 YOGURT CRUNCH: Frozen vanilla yogurt on a waffle cone with granola on top.

#49 YOGURT CRISP: Frozen chocolate yogurt on a waffle cone with crispy rice cereal on top.

#50 DOUBLE DIP: A waffle cone with a small scoop of vanilla ice milk topped by a small scoop of chocolate ice milk.

To eat with a spoon:

#51 PEACHY KEEN: Vanilla ice milk with sliced canned peaches (the kind packed in fruit juice) and some juice from the peach can.

#52 HAWAIIAN TREAT: Chocolate ice milk with canned crushed pineapple and a little of the pineapple juice from the can. (*Don't* use the kind packed in syrup.)

#53 RED AND WHITE: Frozen vanilla yogurt with sliced fresh strawberries.

#54 SKINNY SPLIT: Sliced banana topped by very small scoops of vanilla, chocolate, and strawberry ice milk, with a dab of whipped topping.

#55 MELON BALL: A cantaloupe half with a scoop of frozen vanilla yogurt inside.

#56 CORNY SUNDAE: Sliced banana topped with a scoop of frozen chocolate yogurt and some crushed corn flakes.

M is for MAGNIFICENT SUNDAES

Great Moment in Ice Cream History: Back in the 1890s there were laws in some states that said no ice cream sodas could be sold on Sunday. (They were too sinfully good!) Then someone came up with a clever idea: an ice cream soda *without* the soda — just ice cream and syrup. And that's how the ice cream sundae was born!

#57 MAPLE WALNUT SUNDAE

This is what you get when you cross a maple tree with a walnut tree.

> *You need:*
> 1 scoop vanilla ice cream
> 2 tablespoons maple syrup (or
> maple-flavored syrup)
> 2 tablespoons chopped walnuts
> whipped cream
> 1 walnut half

Put the vanilla ice cream into a dessert bowl. Pour the maple syrup over the ice cream. Sprinkle the chopped walnuts over the syrup and cover with whipped cream. Top with a walnut half. Eat. Makes 1.

#58 HOT FUDGE SUNDAE

The hot fudge sundae may be the most famous sundae of all. This recipe makes enough fudge sauce for 1 large or 2 small sundaes.

You need:

> ¼ cup chocolate chips
> 1 teaspoon hot water
> 1 teaspoon milk
> 1 large scoop vanilla ice cream
> whipped cream
> 1 cherry

To make the sauce:

Put chocolate chips in a small bowl. Put the bowl with the chips in another, larger bowl filled with very hot or boiling water. (Or ask an adult to put the bowl in a frying pan filled with water over low heat.) Stir. When the chips are all melted (they will look shiny when they are melted) take the bowl out of the water. (Use a pot holder since the bowl may be very hot.) Stir in hot water. When mixture is smooth, stir in milk.

To make the sundae:

Put a large scoop of vanilla ice cream in a dessert bowl. Top with hot fudge sauce. Then cover with whipped cream. Stick a cherry on top. Eat. Makes 1.

[Hint: If the fudge sauce thickens and cools too much before you use it, just heat it again, the way you did to melt the chips, and stir until smooth.]

#59 WORTH-A-MINT SUNDAE

Beware! This chocolate mint sauce is *rich*!

You need:

> 1/4 cup heavy (whipping) cream
> 2 large chocolate-covered mint
> patties (1.5 ounces each)
> 3 scoops vanilla ice cream
> peppermint candies, crushed

To make the sauce:

Pour heavy cream into a small saucepan. Unwrap the mint patties. Break them into small pieces and add them to the saucepan. Ask an adult to put the pan over low heat. As the cream begins to heat, the chocolate will begin to melt. Use a pot holder to take the pan from the heat; stir gently. Then put the pan back over the heat. Repeat until the candy is all melted and the sauce is smooth. Let the sauce cool until it is lukewarm.

To make the sundae:

Put 1 scoop of vanilla ice cream into each of 3 dessert bowls. (Or put them all into 1 large bowl if you want to make a giant sundae.) Pour chocolate mint sauce over the ice cream. Sprinkle crushed peppermint candies on top. Serve. Makes 1-3 sundaes.

N is for NUTS AND OTHER CRUNCHY, CANDY TOPPINGS AND MIX-INS

Use these ideas for toppings and mix-ins to invent new sundaes of your own.

If you're mixing in: Before you begin, put the ice cream in a bowl and let it soften a few minutes so that you can stir it — but don't let it get soupy. Sprinkle in your mix and stir it lightly. Then cover and freeze until the ice cream is firm. That should take 30-90 minutes, depending on how cold your freezer is and the amount of ice cream.

#60 NUTT'N DOIN'

Use peanut butter morsels (next to the chocolate chips in the supermarket baking section) and chopped honey-roasted peanuts.

#61 SUPER CRUNCH

Use crushed corn chips and miniature chocolate chips.

#62 SALTY DOG

Use crushed potato chips, chopped peanuts, and chocolate sprinkles (jimmies).

#63 CANDY STORE I

Use a broken crunchy candy bar (like chocolate-coated crispy rice) and candy-coated chocolate pieces.

#64 CANDY STORE II

Use crushed peppermint sticks and a chopped milk chocolate bar.

#65 COOKIE JAR

Use finely crushed vanilla and chocolate sandwich cookies with white filling.

#66 FOR THE BIRDS

Use sunflower seeds, sesame seeds, and raisins.

#67 CHOCOLATE DREAM

Use chocolate-covered raisins, chocolate-covered peanuts, and miniature chocolate chips.

#68 FRUIT SALAD

Use canned fruit salad that you have drained and dried on paper towels (or fresh fruit cut into bite-sized pieces), and chopped walnuts.

O is for OLD-FASHIONED SODA PARLOR TREATS

Before there were shopping malls and fast-food restaurants, there were ice cream parlors. People of all ages would head to the parlor for a sundae, a milk shake, or a float and a chance to meet friends and hear the latest news. Every town had its ice cream parlor or its drugstore with a soda fountain. Many of the recipes you've seen already are soda fountain treats. Here are some more!

#69 HOBOKEN

Hoboken is a city in New Jersey, but you can eat this sundae anywhere you like.

You need:

2 scoops chocolate ice cream
½ cup crushed pineapple
    packed in heavy syrup
a dollop of whipped cream

Put chocolate ice cream into a dessert bowl. Spoon on plenty of crushed pineapple, plus the syrup it is packed in. Top with whipped cream. Eat. Makes 1.

#70 TIN ROOF

For this sundae you need red-skinned Spanish peanuts. If you can't find them, use whole roasted peanuts, preferably unsalted.

You need:

2 scoops vanilla ice cream
2-3 tablespoons chocolate
    syrup
1-2 tablespoons Spanish
    peanuts

Put vanilla ice cream into a dessert bowl. Pour on chocolate syrup and top with Spanish peanuts. Eat. Makes 1.

P is for PARTY

What's a party without ice cream? It certainly isn't cool. Try one of these ideas the next time you're celebrating with a crowd.

#71 VANILLA FUDGE PCs
(Personal Cupcakes)

These Personal Cupcakes are like mini ice cream cakes.
You need:

> 12 chocolate cupcakes
> about ¾ cup vanilla ice cream,
>   soft enough to spread
> chocolate syrup
> ½ can chocolate frosting

If the cupcakes were baked in paper wrappers, take the paper off. Put clean cupcake wrappers into the cups of a 12-muffin tin. Make room for the tin in your freezer.

Cut 1 cupcake in half and fit the bottom half into one of the cupcake wrappers. Spread about 2 or 3 teaspoons vanilla ice cream over the bottom half of the cupcake. Make an even layer that covers the cake.

Pour about 1 teaspoon chocolate syrup over the ice cream and spread it evenly with the back of a spoon.

Put the top of the cupcake over the syrup. Press down gently. Top with chocolate frosting. Repeat with remaining cupcakes. Freeze until firm, at least 1 hour. Serve, or cover with plastic wrap or foil and keep in freezer until ready to serve. Makes 12.

#72 FRUITY PCs

Follow the directions for VANILLA FUDGE PCs, but make these changes: The cupcakes should be yellow; the ice cream should be strawberry; use apricot or other fruit preserves instead of chocolate syrup; and top with vanilla frosting covered with rainbow sprinkles.

#73 SEND IN THE CLOWNS

Your guests can really clown around with these!

You need:

> scoops of ice cream
> sugar cones
> cans of icing or whipped cream
> decorations: little candies,
>   raisins, chocolate chips, nuts

Give everyone a scoop of ice cream on a plate. Stick the ice cream cone over the ice cream, like a pointed hat. Now get artistic — quickly, before the ice cream melts! Make faces on the ice cream and decorate the cone hat using whipped cream, icing, and decorations. Admire your work. Then, eat *immediately!*

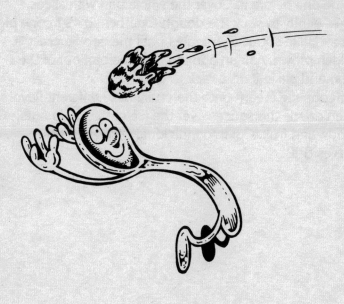

#74 FROZEN PIZZA

No cheese, no sauce, no pepperoni — just tons of ice cream. Everyone can help make this pie!

You need:

> 1 20-ounce roll refrigerator
>   sugar cookie dough, frozen
> 10-12 scoops ice cream
> chocolate, marshmallow, and
>   butterscotch sauces
> nuts, fruit, candy

Ask an adult to preheat the oven to 375 degrees. Line a 14-inch pizza pan (or a cookie sheet) with aluminum foil. Cut the cookie dough into slices about ¼-inch thick. Starting along the outer edge of the pan, put the slices on the pan in a circle, letting each slice cover a *little* bit of the one before it. Cover the whole pan with slices. Press gently to stick the dough together so it's in one big piece. Bake about 10 minutes until the cookie crust is golden brown. Ask an adult to take the pan out of the oven and place it on a rack to cool.

Scoop ice cream onto the crust. (Use different flavors.) Then drizzle the sauces over the ice cream. Add nuts, candy, and fruit. Cut into individual slices and eat. Serves 8-10.

#75 ASSEMBLY-LINE SUNDAES

This recipe is perfect for a crowd. Your guests can have exactly what they want on these sundaes.

You need:

> 2-3 ice cream flavors
> bowls of toppings, as many as
> you like: chocolate,
> marshmallow, butterscotch,
> chopped nuts, chopped
> peanut brittle, sliced or chunk
> fruit, broken cookies,
> chopped candy bars,
> sprinkles, broken pretzels,
> sliced bananas,
> marshmallows, granola,
> coconut, chocolate chips,
> whipped cream, cherries

Let each guest take a bowl, fill it with ice cream, and make the most wild, gooey, crunchy sundae possible. Eat right away. Makes a lot.

Q is for
QUICK COMBOS

You can make these treats *fast*, and you probably have what you need in the house right now.

#76 DUSTY CONE: Dip a vanilla or chocolate ice cream cone into some powdered chocolate or strawberry milk flavoring. Fill with your favorite flavor ice cream.

#77 SAUCY CREAM: Cover a scoop of vanilla ice cream with a spoonful of applesauce. Sprinkle on some cinnamon and a dash of ground cloves.

#78 FLORIDA COOLER: Put 2 scoops of vanilla ice cream in a glass. Cover with orange juice.

#79 COCONUT SNOW: Pour chocolate syrup over any flavor ice cream. Cover with flaked coconut.

#80 ICE CREAM CRUMBLE: Break a slice of date-nut bread or other fruit bread into pieces. Put pieces of bread in a bowl and cover with a scoop of vanilla or chocolate ice cream.

R is for REALLY SPECIAL OCCASIONS

Some people would argue that ice cream is always special. But these creations are extra-special because they take a little more work.

#81 PEANUT CREAM DREAM

You can make this pie with vanilla or chocolate ice cream.

You need:

> 1 pint chocolate or vanilla ice cream
> 1 graham cracker or chocolate cookie crumb pie crust
> ¾ cup chopped peanuts
> ½ cup marshmallow cream
> ½ cup peanut butter
> 1 cup heavy (whipping) cream

If the ice cream is very hard, put it in the refrigerator for 10-15 minutes to soften slightly. Spread the ice cream in the bottom of the pie crust. Smooth the top. Sprinkle ½ cup chopped peanuts over the ice cream. (You'll use the rest of the nuts later.) Place in freezer.

Put the marshmallow cream and peanut butter into a small mixing bowl. Ask an adult to blend them with an electric mixer. (Don't worry if the mixture sticks to the blades.) Add about 1 tablespoon of the heavy cream and keep mixing. Continue to add the heavy cream, 1 tablespoon at a time, until you have added the whole cup. If lumps of marshmallow and peanut butter form on the sides of the bowl or on the mixer blades, stop the mixer and scrape the lumps into the bowl. Mix until smooth and creamy.

Pour the peanut cream mixture over the nuts and ice cream in the pie shell. Sprinkle the last ¼ cup of nuts over the top. Freeze 2-3 hours, or until very firm. Serve. Makes 6-10 servings.

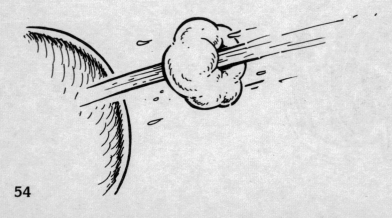

#82 BOMBES AWAY

A bombe is a special mold for making a layered ice cream dessert. If you don't have a bombe, you can use a metal bowl. (If your bowl is bigger than 1 quart, you'll need more ice cream and a longer freezing time.)

> ***You need:***
> > 1 pint each of 2 different colors
> > of ice cream, such as
> > strawberry and pistachio, or
> > chocolate and vanilla
> > 1 cup of sherbet (different color
> > from your ice cream choices)

Put your metal bowl in the freezer. Choose which ice cream you want for the outer layer. Put it in the refrigerator for 15 minutes to soften.

Spread the outer-layer ice cream in the chilled metal bowl. (Work quickly!) Cover the whole inside of the bowl. Try to make an even layer. Put a sheet of plastic wrap over the ice cream and freeze for 30 minutes.

After 15 minutes, put your second ice cream choice in the refrigerator to soften. Wait 15 minutes. Take the bowl

out of the freezer and remove the plastic wrap. Spread the second ice cream over the first. Make a smooth even layer. The space in the middle should hold about a cup of sherbet. (If you have too much ice cream, don't use it all.) Cover with plastic wrap and freeze for 30 minutes.

After 20 minutes, put the sherbet in the refrigerator to soften. Wait 10 minutes. Take the bowl out of the freezer and remove the plastic wrap. Then fill the space in the middle with sherbet. Smooth the surface. Cover with plastic wrap and freeze until firm, at least 1 hour.

To free the bombe from the bowl, dip the bowl into warm water up to its edge for 5-10 seconds. (Don't let the water run into the ice cream!) Turn it upside down onto a chilled plate. Cut into slices and serve.
Makes 6-8 servings.

S is for SHAKES

Fast-food restaurants usually serve "thick shakes." They're almost pure ice cream and so thick, you can barely drink them with a straw. A real old-fashioned milk shake is thinner. It's made of milk, ice cream, and flavorings all whirled together.

You can shake, rattle, and roll these drinks in a milk shake machine, if you have one. Or, use a wire whisk or a spoon. (A blender can make the shake too thin.) Stir very well to mix in the ice cream and make the drink frothy, but don't blend the ice cream completely.

#83 CLASSIC CHOCOLATE MILK SHAKE

Pour 2-4 tablespoons chocolate syrup into a tall glass. Add ½ cup milk and stir well. Add 2-3 scoops vanilla ice cream. Blend in the ice cream to make the drink frothy. Serve right away. Makes 1 tall drink.

#84 CLASSIC VANILLA MILK SHAKE

Ask an adult to put 2 tablespoons boiling water in a mug or a small bowl. Add ¼ cup sugar to the water. Stir very well for about 1 minute, until the sugar is dissolved. Add 1 tablespoon vanilla extract. Stir.

Pour 2-4 tablespoons of this vanilla syrup into a tall glass. Add ½ cup milk and stir. Add 2-3 scoops vanilla ice cream. Blend in the ice cream to make the drink frothy. Serve right away. Makes 1 tall drink.

#85 BLUE MOON

Put 1 cup fresh or frozen blueberries into a blender. (If they are fresh, wash them first and dry on a paper towel.) Add 1 cup milk and ask a grown-up to whirl the mixture until the blueberries are in small pieces. Add 3 large scoops vanilla ice cream and whirl until the mixture is soupy but still thick. To make the berries taste berrier, stir in ½ teaspoon lemon juice. Pour into a very tall glass and drink. Makes 1 large or 2 medium purple shakes, very thick and full of blueberry bits.

#86 PINK FLAMINGO

Put 1 cup fresh or frozen strawberries into a blender. (If they are fresh, wash them first and dry on a paper towel.) Add 1 cup milk and ask a grown-up to whirl the mixture until the berries are crushed. Add 3 large scoops strawberry ice cream and whirl until the shake is thin enough to pour out of the blender. Pour into a tall glass (or 2 smaller ones) and dig in. Makes 1 or 2.

#87 A-PEELING BANANA SHAKE

Peel 2 large or 4 small ripe bananas. Break the bananas into several pieces. Seal them in a plastic bag and freeze until very firm, at least 2 hours.

Put the frozen banana pieces into a blender. Add 1 cup milk and ask a grown-up to blend until the bananas are completely chopped up. You may have to stop the blender and push the banana pieces down with a rubber spatula. Add 1-2 scoops vanilla ice cream and whirl just to mix. Drink. Makes 1 tall shake.

T is for
TAKE-ALONG TREATS

Take these ice cream treats with you . . . but don't expect them to stick around for long!

#88 PEANUT BUTTER FUDGE HOLE-IN-ONE

Try *this* peanut butter cup. It's got ice cream in the middle!

You need:

> 1 plain donut (the cake type is best)
> 1 tablespoon peanut butter
> 1 tablespoon hot fudge topping from a jar (or any thick chocolate sauce)
> 2-4 tablespoons chocolate ice cream

Ask an adult to slice the donut in half so that you have 2 circles. Spread the cut side of one half with peanut butter. Spread the cut side of the other half with hot fudge topping (don't heat it up first). Spoon chocolate ice cream over the peanut butter. Top with the hot fudge side of the donut. Eat or wrap tightly in plastic wrap and freeze. Makes 1.

#89 FEEL-YOUR-OATS SANDWICH

You need:

> 2 oatmeal cookies
> vanilla ice cream
> granola

Spread the vanilla ice cream over the back of one oat-meal cookie. Top with another cookie. Spread a few teaspoons of granola on wax paper or a plate. Roll the edges of the sandwich in the granola. Eat right away or wrap tightly in plastic wrap and freeze. Makes 1.

    [Hint: For these sandwich recipes you'll need spreadable ice cream. To soften ice cream so that it's spreadable, let it sit out at room temperature for 5-10 minutes. Don't let it get soupy!]

#90 FEELING CHIPPER SANDWICH

You need:

> 2 chocolate chip cookies
> chocolate ice cream
> miniature chocolate chips

Follow the directions for making FEEL-YOUR-OATS SANDWICH, using these ingredients.

#91 IN-THE-PINK SANDWICH

You need:

> 2 sugar cookies
> strawberry ice cream
> red-tinted sugar (sold in baking
>   sections of supermarkets)

Follow the directions for making FEEL-YOUR-OATS SANDWICH, using these ingredients.

#92 GOING NUTTY SANDWICH

You need:

> 2 peanut butter cookies
> chocolate ice cream
> chopped peanuts

Follow the directions for making FEEL-YOUR-OATS SANDWICH, using these ingredients.

U is for
UNUSUALLY GOOD

#93 APPLEBERRY COOLER

Get ready for fruity and fizzy!

You need:

>   2-4 tablespoons frozen apple
>   juice concentrate
>   club soda or seltzer
>   1-2 scoops strawberry ice
>   cream

Put the frozen apple juice concentrate into a glass. Add a few tablespoons club soda or seltzer and stir well. Add 1-2 scoops strawberry ice cream. Fill the glass with club soda or seltzer. Stir gently. Drink. Makes 1.

#94 FINGER SNAPPER

This spicy ice cream treat is guaranteed to get your fingers snapping and toes tapping!

You need:

> 1 scoop vanilla ice cream
> 3-6 ginger snaps (cookies)
> waffle or sugar cone
> chocolate sprinkles (jimmies)

Let the vanilla ice cream soften slightly so that you can mash it easily. Meanwhile, ask a grown up to whirl the ginger snaps in a blender or food processor (or put them in a plastic bag and crush them with a rolling pin). You need 3 tablespoons cookie crumbs.

Add the crumbs to the ice cream. Stir gently to mix. Try not to melt the ice cream. Freeze 30 minutes or until firm. Scoop the ice cream onto a cone. Cover with chocolate sprinkles and eat. Makes 1.

#95 ORANGE BLOSSOM

If you're having a gray day, this drink will brighten it up.
You need:

> ½ cup orange juice
> ¼ cup milk
> 1-2 scoops vanilla ice cream

Pour the orange juice and milk into a blender container or a mixing bowl. Add 1 scoop vanilla ice cream. Ask a grown-up to blend the mixture or whisk it yourself until it is frothy. Taste it. If it's not sweet enough for you, add up to 1 scoop more ice cream. Then blend or whisk again. Drink. Makes 1.

V is for VANILLA

#96 POLAR BEAR IN A SNOWSTORM

This bear doesn't bite.

You need:

> 2 scoops vanilla ice cream
> 1-2 tablespoons marshmallow
>   topping
> 1-2 tablespoons flaked coconut

Put 2 scoops of vanilla ice cream into a dessert bowl. Pour on marshmallow topping. (If the topping is too thick, thin it with a few drops of water or milk.) Sprinkle on flaked coconut. Eat. Makes 1.

#97 CHERRY VANILLA LICKS

Give your tongue a treat with these creamy pops!

You need:

1 14-ounce can sweetened
  condensed milk (not
  evaporated milk)
2 6-ounce containers (or 1½
  8-ounce containers) cherry
  yogurt
1 teaspoon vanilla extract
5 paper or plastic cups
5 ice-pop sticks or plastic
  spoons

In a mixing bowl, stir together the condensed milk and cherry yogurt. Add the vanilla extract and stir. Pour mixture into 5 paper or plastic cups. Stick an ice-pop stick or a plastic spoon in the center of each cup. Freeze 2 hours or until firm. To unmold, dip cup into warm water for 5-10 seconds and pull on stick. Makes 5.

W is for WAFFLES AND PANCAKES

#98 BELGIAN WINTER WAFFLES

Most people serve Belgian waffles with whipped cream.
But these waffles are a lot cooler than that!

You need:

> **2 frozen waffles**
> **2 small scoops vanilla ice cream**
> **1 cup sliced strawberries**

Ask an adult to help you toast or microwave the waffles.
Top each with a small scoop of vanilla ice cream. Cover
with sliced strawberries. Eat right away. Makes 1.

#99 WAFFLE SCHOONER

Try this hot fudge sundae — on a raft!

You need:

>1 frozen waffle
>2 scoops vanilla ice cream
>2-3 tablespoons fudge sauce
>from a jar (or make your own:
>see #58 HOT FUDGE
>SUNDAE)

Ask an adult to help you toast or microwave the waffle. Meanwhile, make or heat some fudge sauce. Top the waffle with a scoop of vanilla ice cream. Cover with fudge sauce. Dig in. Makes 1.

#100 FLAPJACK STACKS

Imagine ice cream for breakfast . . . you'd never oversleep again! (These are also good for dessert.)

You need:

> 2 tablespoons maple syrup
> 1 teaspoon butter
> 2 or 3 hot pancakes
> small scoop vanilla ice cream

Put the maple syrup in a very small saucepan. Add 1 teaspoon butter. Have an adult heat the mixture gently, stirring, until the butter is all melted.

Put 2 or 3 hot pancakes on a plate. Top with a small scoop of vanilla ice cream. Pour warm syrup over the ice cream and eat. Makes 1.

X is for X-TRA ATTRACTION

This word search is full of ice creamy delights. Check the list below for the tasty treats hidden inside the box of letters. The words run down, across, and diagonally. Circle the words as you find them. To find the answer to the riddle, write down, in order, the letters that are left. (Start with the letters in the top row and move left to right.)

butterscotch
cherry
chocolate
cone
ice cream soda
marshmallow
milk
nuts

seltzer
shake
split
sprinkle
strawberry
sundae
syrup
vanilla

How do you make an elephant float?
Answer: ___ ___ ___   ___ ___ ___ ___   ___

___ ___ ___ ___ ___   ___ ___ ___ ___

___ ___ ___ ___ ___ ___ ___ ___

___ ___ ___ ___ ___ ___   ___ ___ ___

___ ___ ___ ___   ___ ___ ___   ___ ___ ___

___ ___   ___ ___ ___ ___ ___ ___ ___ ___ ___ !

```
Y I O S T R A W B E R R Y
B C C H O C O L A T E U M
U E V F S I C L N L A G A
T C L A U S O T U S W R
T R I T N H N I N C T E S
E E H C O I L D C E L S H
R A O H L P L A A K T R M
S M E E S S Y L N E E E A
C S R R U P A I A Z K N L
O O D R S O R D T A A A L
T D N Y D P A L H D D A O
C A N E S L E S E P H A W
H M I L K S N S Y R U P T
```

Answers next page

Answer: <u>YOU</u> <u>FILL</u> <u>A</u>
<u>GLASS</u> <u>WITH</u>
<u>CHOCOLATE</u>
<u>SYRUP</u> <u>AND</u>
<u>SODA</u> <u>AND</u> <u>ADD</u>
<u>AN</u> <u>ELEPHANT</u>!

Y is for
YOUR CREATIONS

Use this section to jot down your own concoctions.
When it comes to ice cream, anyone can create
scrumptious combinations!

_____

_____

_____

_____

_____

_____

_____

_____

_____

_____

_____

_____

_____

_____

_____

_____

_____

Z is for
ZEBRA PARFAITS

A parfait should be served in a tall narrow glass to show off the layers.

#101 ANYTHING GOES PARFAIT

You pick the ingredients for this one!
> *You need:*
>> about 1 cup ice cream
>> whipped cream
>> 3 different colors of syrup or topping, such as brown (chocolate), red (chopped cherries or strawberries), and yellow (pineapple)
>>> OR
>> 3 different colors of ice cream and only 1 topping

Put a heaping tablespoon of ice cream in the bottom of a tall glass. Cover with a topping. Add another dollop of ice cream and another helping of topping. Then add another layer of ice cream and one more topping. Finish off with whipped cream and eat with a long spoon. Makes 1.